Trace Lines

To Parents: In this activity, your child will practice drawing short horizontal lines. When your child is ready to use crayons after tracing, have them use crayons that are easy to color with. Children of this age usually do not apply much pressure when writing.

Trace lines from ➡ to ➡. Put the stickers on 🐙 🐙.

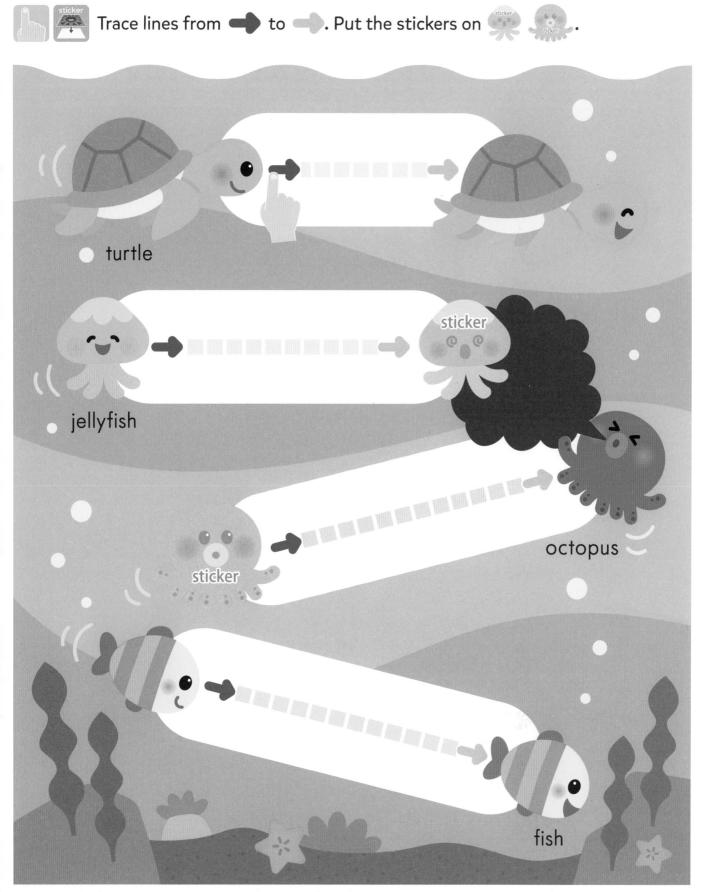

turtle

jellyfish

sticker

sticker

octopus

fish

Bonus Challenge! Point to each animal and say its name.

2

Color the Fruit

 Color each fruit with its matching color.

apple

grape

orange

strawberry

banana

Bonus Challenge! Point to each fruit and say its name.

Get Dressed

To Parents: While turning the cards over, point out the important elements of getting dressed, such as the front and back of clothes, the holes for the child's head and arms, and how to put on pants one leg at a time. This will help your child learn to get dressed independently.

Follow the instructions to dress the cat.

Sticker

★ Good job! ★

How do I get dressed?

• How to Make •

Cut the gray line and fold the dotted line.

1. This is a T-shirt. These are shorts.
2. This is a T-shirt. Let's check the front side of the shirt and put it on.
   Fold
   Fold
3. Let's sit down and put on shorts.
   Can you get dressed well?
   Finished

• How to Play •

1. Can you get dressed well?
   Open
2. This is a T-shirt. Let's check the front side of the shirt and put it on.
   Open
3. This is a T-shirt. These are shorts.
   Open
   Let's sit down and put on shorts.
4. This is a T-shirt. These are shorts. This is a jacket.
   I did it!

This is a T-shirt.

Fold up

These are shorts.

Fold up

This is a jacket.

Fold up

I did it!

Foldout Picture Book

Fold down

Can you get dressed well?

Fold down

Let's check the front side of the shirt and put it on.

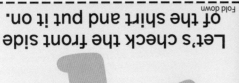

Fold down

Let's sit down and put on shorts.

Match the Treat

To Parents: Guide your child by pointing to the cupcake and saying, "Look at the color of the cupcake's frosting. Find another treat that looks the same."

 Find a treat that matches the one in the example and color the ◯.

Sticker

Good job!

example

Match the Monsters

To Parents: This activity focuses on observation skills. Ask your child to point to their favorite monster. Then ask if they can find the same monster elsewhere.

Draw a line to connect the matching monsters.

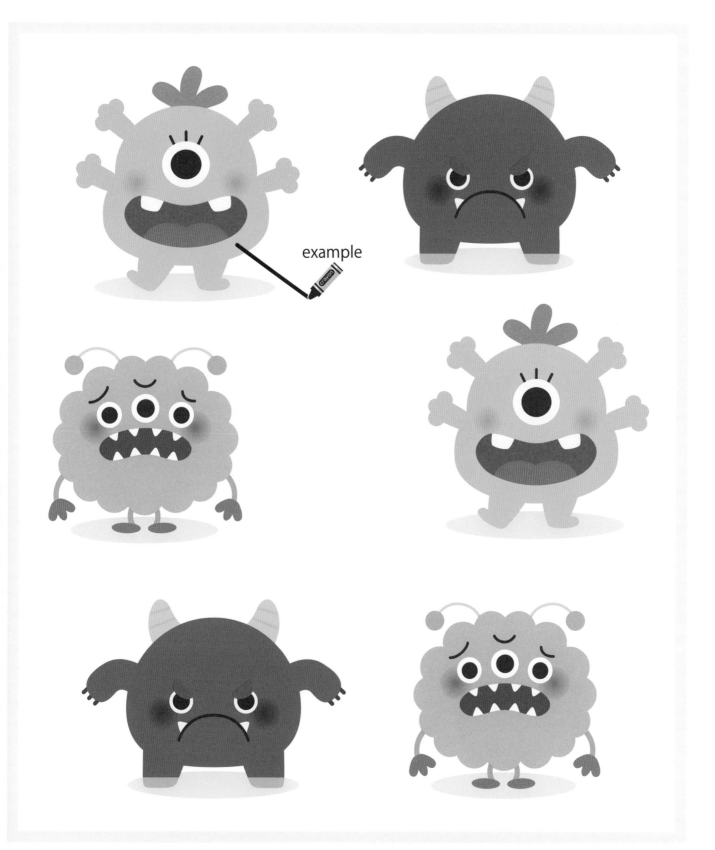

example

Bonus Challenge! Find the angry monsters and point to them.

Trace the Letter A

To Parents: Trace the letter with your finger, following the numbers and arrows. Hold your child's finger and help them trace the letter.

 Trace the A and say "A." Put stickers on that start with the letter A.

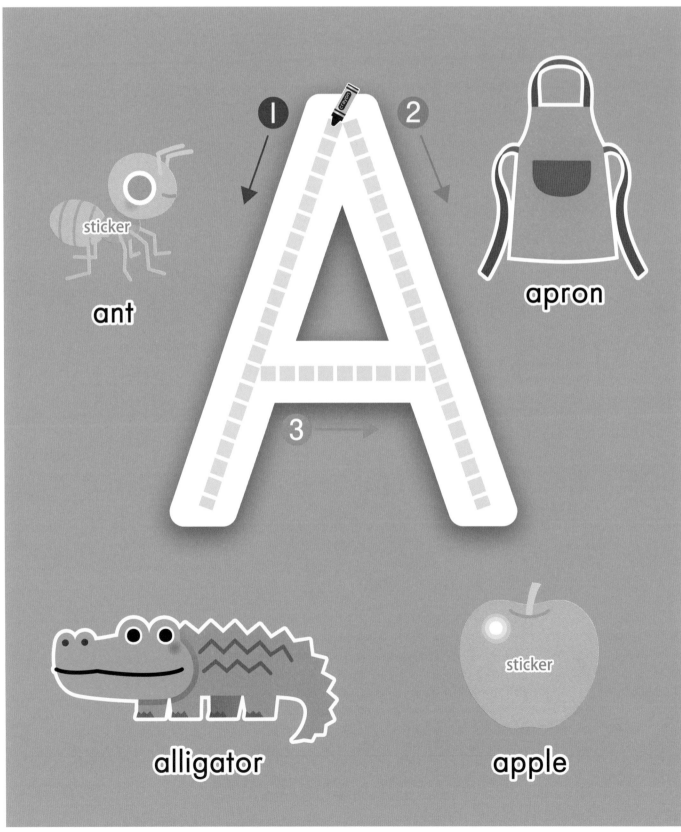

sticker

ant

apron

alligator

apple

Bonus Challenge! Point to each object and say its name.

Trace the Letter B

To Parents: Hold your child's finger and help them trace the letter. Then name the letter and the objects on this page, noting that they begin with B.

 Trace the B and say "B." Put stickers on  that start with the letter B.

bee

banana

sticker

bear

sticker

bus

Bonus Challenge! Point to each object and say its name.

Trace the Letter C

To Parents: Fold along the dotted line for your child at first. Do it from the left side to the right side. Then let your child close and open the paper to enjoy how the picture changes. Say to your child, "Look at the C! Cat starts with C."

Trace a line from ➡ to ➡. Then fold along the – – – and —·— lines.

How to Play

cat

Fold down

Fold up

Bonus Challenge! Find the cat with the heart pattern and point to it.

Trace the Letter D

To Parents: Fold from the right side to the left side this time. While closing and opening, say to your child, "Look at the D! Dog starts with D."

Sticker

Good job!

Trace a line from ➡ to ➡. Then fold along the - - - and —·— lines.

Fold

How to Play

dog

Fold up

Fold down

Bonus Challenge! Find the dog with black spots and point to it.

Trace the Letter E

To Parents: Give your child a clue to what's hiding behind the letter by saying, "The animal's nose is long." Then say, "Elephant starts with E."

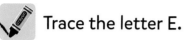 Trace the letter E.

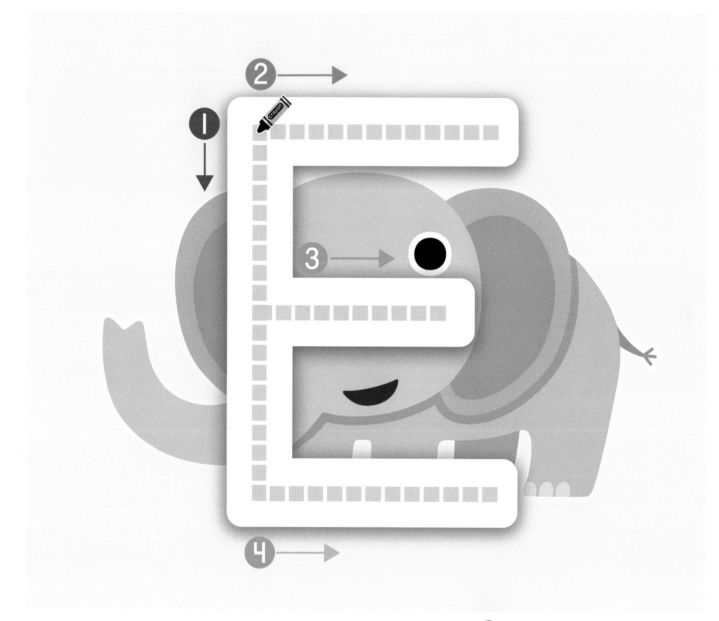

 What's hiding behind the letter E?
Put a sticker on the ⬤.

sticker

Go to the Bathroom

To Parents: This activity helps to develop awareness of potty training. When done, say to your child, "Do you have to go to the potty?" and "You should go to the potty before you go out." This will show your child how to go to the bathroom independently.

Sticker

Good job!

Move the bear from ➡ to ➡ and help him sit on the toilet.

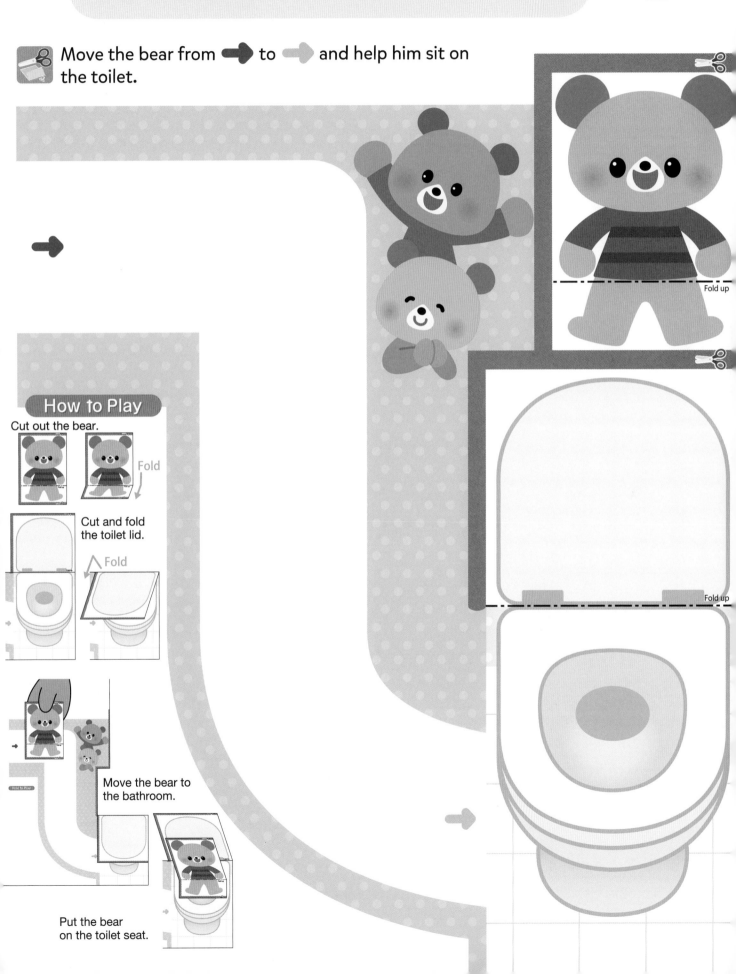

How to Play

Cut out the bear.

Fold

Cut and fold the toilet lid.

Fold

Move the bear to the bathroom.

Put the bear on the toilet seat.

Fold up

Fold up

Find the Different Juice

To Parents: In this activity, your child will practice comparing different objects. Ask your child, "Which glass of juice is different from the others?"

 One glass of juice is different from the others. Find it and color the ◯.

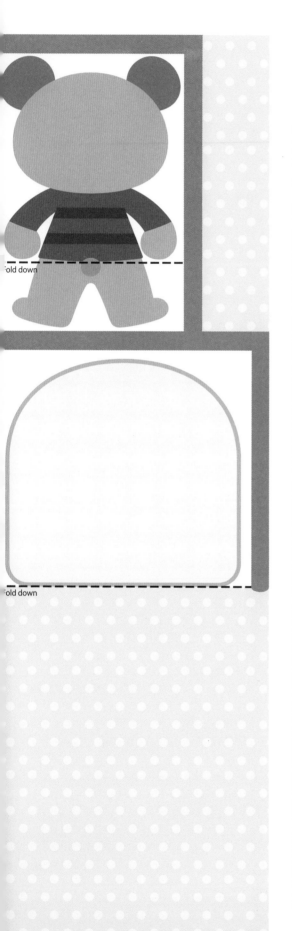

Draw Lines

To Parents: In this activity, your child will practice drawing curved and jagged lines. If it seems difficult, put your hand on your child's to help them draw.

 Draw lines from ➡ to ➡.

example

Bonus Challenge! Draw cactus thorns with a green crayon.

● For page 14

glue

Match the Red Object

To Parents: This activity helps develop color recognition. After gluing, let your child say, "A fire truck is red."

 Cut out the fire truck below and glue it onto its matching shadow.

red

apple

strawberry

tomato

ladybug

paste

fire truck

crab

red

white · red · orange · yellow · green · blue · purple · black

Bonus Challenge! Say the name of each crayon's color.

Match the Green Object

To Parents: Let your child say, "A zucchini is green," "A leaf is green," and so on until they've named all the objects.

Sticker
Good job!

 Cut out the alligator below and glue it onto its matching shadow.

green

zucchini

leaf

tree

paste

alligator

frog

green

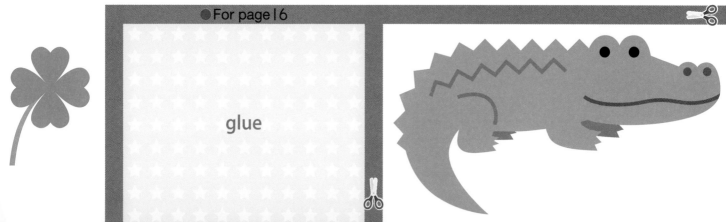

● For page 16

glue

Match the Blue Object

To Parents: What kind of things are blue? Encourage speaking and color recognition by finding more blue things around your home.

 Cut out the sky below and glue it onto its matching shadow.

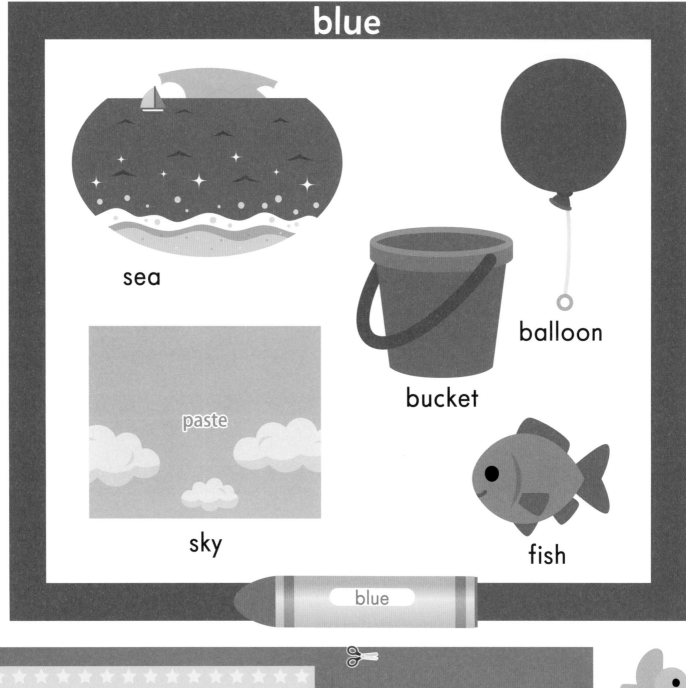

blue

sea

balloon

bucket

paste

sky

fish

blue

glue

Color with Yellow

To Parents: Don't worry if your child colors outside the shapes. It is more important that they select the right color.

 Color each object with its matching color.

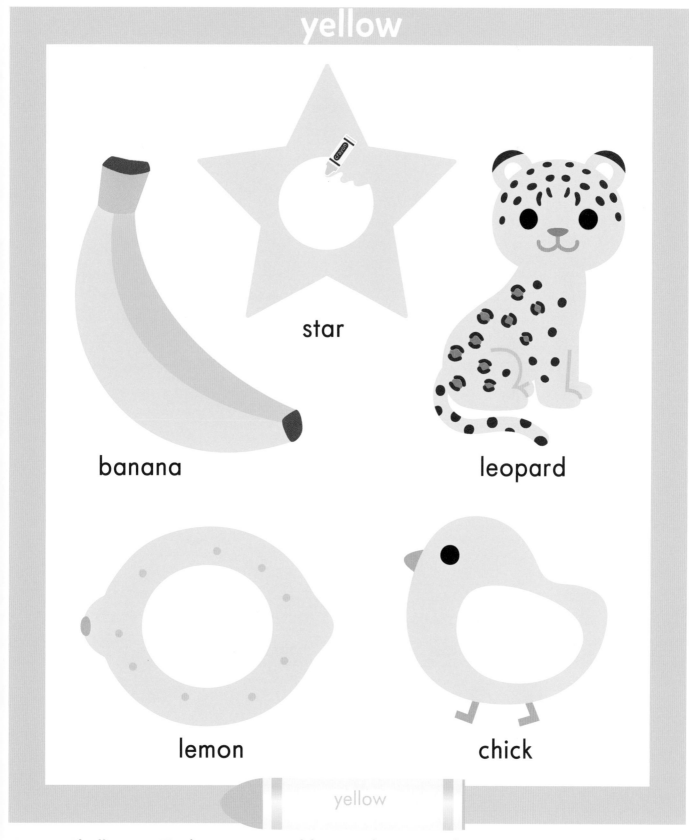

yellow

star

banana

leopard

lemon

chick

yellow

Bonus Challenge! Find two pieces of fruit and point to them.

Color with Orange

To Parents: After your child finishes coloring, ask them to name the objects. This will enhance color recognition skills.

Color each object with its matching color.

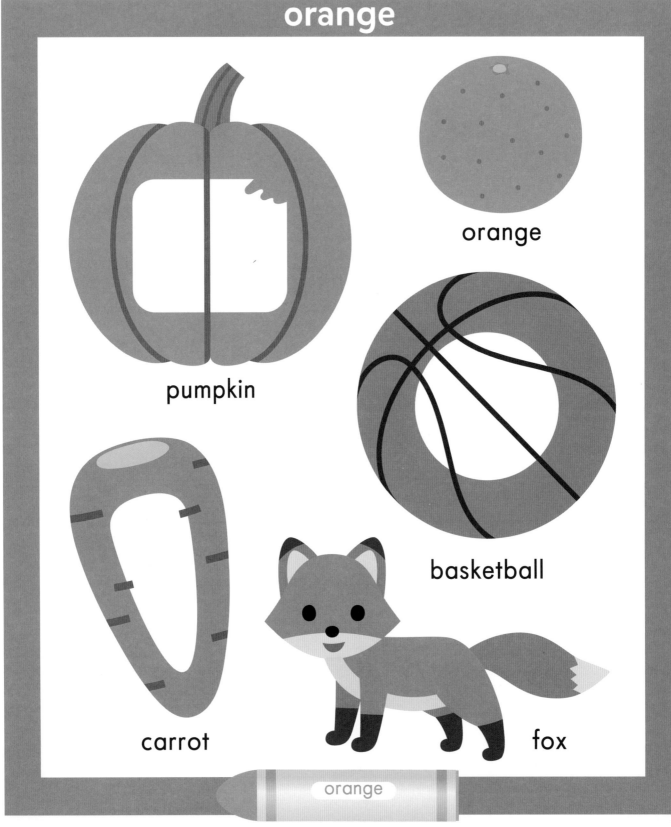

orange

orange

pumpkin

basketball

carrot

fox

orange

Bonus Challenge! Find the animal and point to it.

Color with Purple

To Parents: After your child finishes coloring, ask them to point to something nearby that is the same color as the eggplant and grapes.

 Color each object with its matching color.

purple

eggplant

grapes

plum

pansy

purple

Bonus Challenge! Find the flower and point to it.

Pretend to Be Vegetables

To Parents: This activity helps develop imagination and expression. Use your whole body and pretend to be a vegetable with your child. When done with this activity, pretend to be more vegetables, such as a potato and an eggplant.

Pretend to be a vegetable using your whole body!

Be a cucumber!

Put your hands up and stretch them.

Be broccoli!

Put your hands up and shake them in the air.

Be a pumpkin!

Raise your hands together above your head while sitting.

Play with Cards

To Parents: This activity helps children deduce an object from its shadow. Encourage your child to remember the names of animals, food, clothes, and tableware, too.

 Play card games!
Follow the instructions on page 29.

giraffe

elephant

koala

bear

Play with Cards

To Parents: Cut out the cards from pages 21 to 28.

Play with Cards

To Parents: Cut out the cards from pages 21 to 28.

 Play card games!
Follow the instructions on page 29.

monkey

rabbit

banana

strawberry

Play with Cards

To Parents: Cut out the cards from pages 21 to 28.

Play with Cards

To Parents: Cut out the cards from pages 21 to 28.

Play card games!
Follow the instructions on page 29.

watermelon

grapes

T-shirt

socks

Play with Cards

To Parents: Cut out the cards from pages 21 to 28.

Play with Cards

To Parents: Cut out the cards from pages 21 to 28.

Sticker
Good job!

 Play card games!
Cut out the cards and card holder. Then follow the instructions on page 29.

cup

spoon

Fold down

paste ②

Card Holder

paste ③

Fold down

Fold down

paste ❶

Play with Cards

To Parents: Cut out the cards from pages 21 to 28.

Play with Cards

To Parents: While playing the shadow game, give your child a clue by saying, "This animal has a long nose and big ears" or "This animal climbs trees." Play the next game by flipping the cards slowly at first, and then speeding up the pace. When done, encourage your child to put the cards away independently.

 Play card games!

Guess the Shadow

Show a shadow card and ask your child to guess what object it is.

What is this shadow?

Elephant!

Flash Cards

Flip the cards and ask your child to say the names of the objects, matching the speed of the flipping cards.

Monkey!

Elephant!

Spoon!

Grapes!

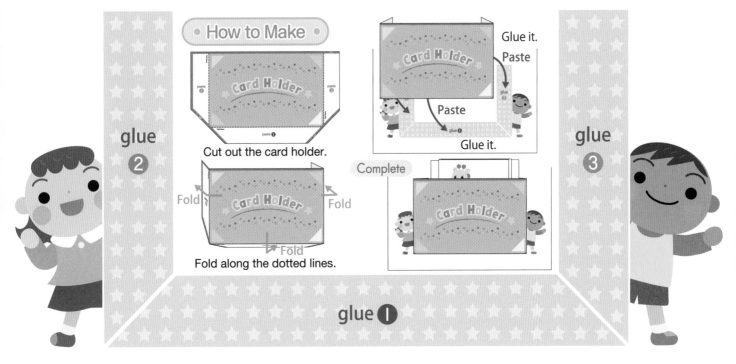

glue ②

glue ③

• How to Make •

Cut out the card holder.

Fold along the dotted lines.

Glue it.
Paste
Paste
Glue it.

Complete

glue ①

Match the Parts

Draw a line from each part of a dinosaur shown in a circle below to the whole dinosaur it's part of.

example

Find the Hidden Eggs

To Parents: When your child is looking for eggs, give them a clue by saying, "It's under the feet of the blue dinosaur." When all the eggs are found, encourage your child to count them.

Bonus Challenge! Find five eggs in the pictures on pages 30 and 31 and circle them.

Name Colors

To Parents: When the game is done, point to each color while saying its name. Then have your child point to the colors while you name them!

 Play color games.

① Say the name of each color. Ask your child to find the color and point to it.

Which is orange?

② Say the names of two colors. Ask your child to find the colors and point to them with both hands.

Point to blue and green.

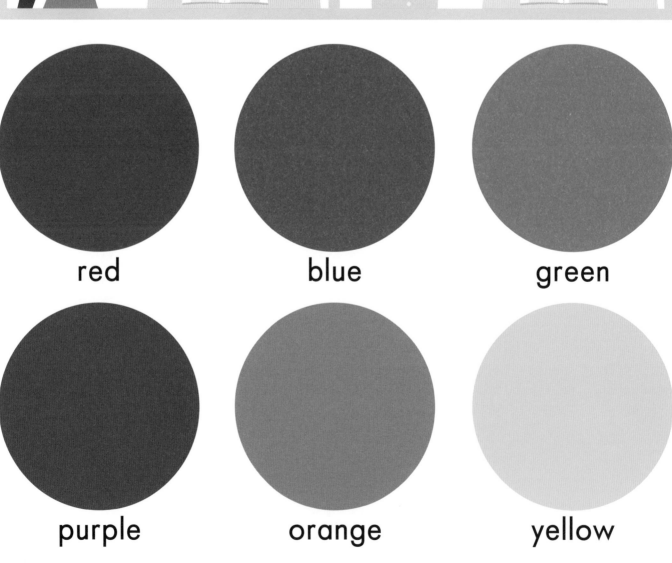

red

blue

green

purple

orange

yellow

Trace the Triangle

To Parents: After your child draws the lines, say, "A slice of pizza is a triangle." This will help them remember the shape.

Trace lines from ➡ to ➡. Then put the green peppers, tomato, pepperoni, and cheese on the pizza.

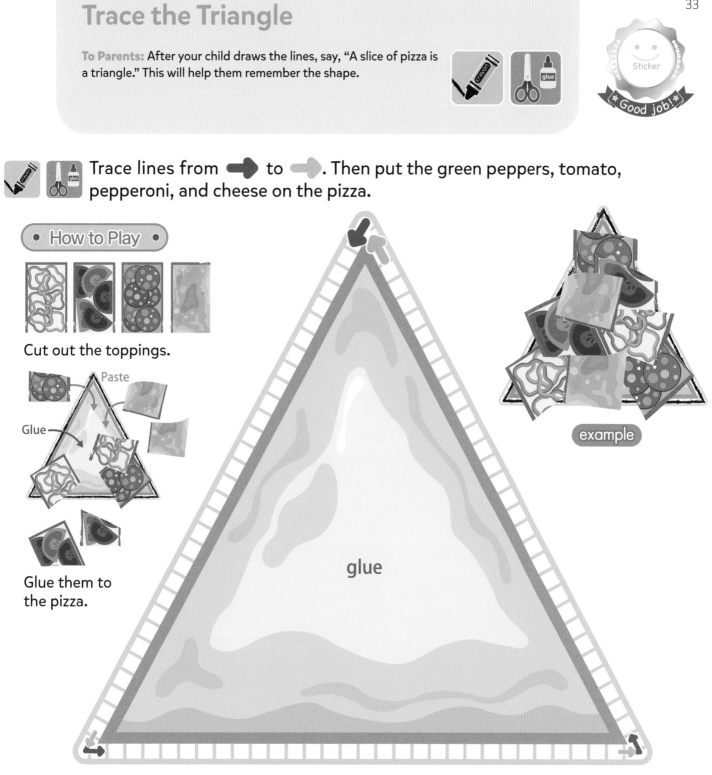

• How to Play •

Cut out the toppings.

Paste

Glue

Glue them to the pizza.

glue

example

34

Trace the Square

To Parents: After your child draws the lines, say, "A blanket is a square." This will help them remember the shape.

 Trace lines from ➡ to ➡. Find the giraffes and put the 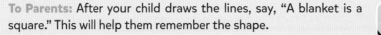 stickers on them.

Bonus Challenge! Count the bears and rabbits.

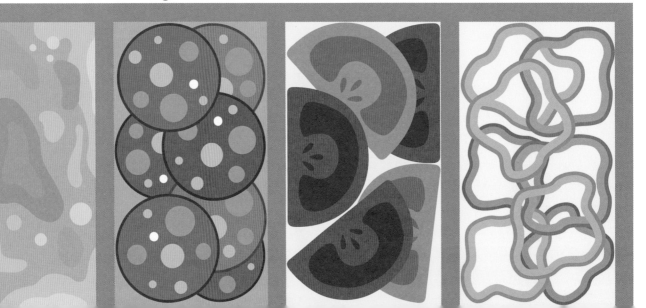

Trace the Circle

To Parents: After your child draws the line, say, "A frying pan is a circle." This will help them remember the shape.

Sticker

Good job!

Trace lines from ➡ to ➡. Then make a pancake.

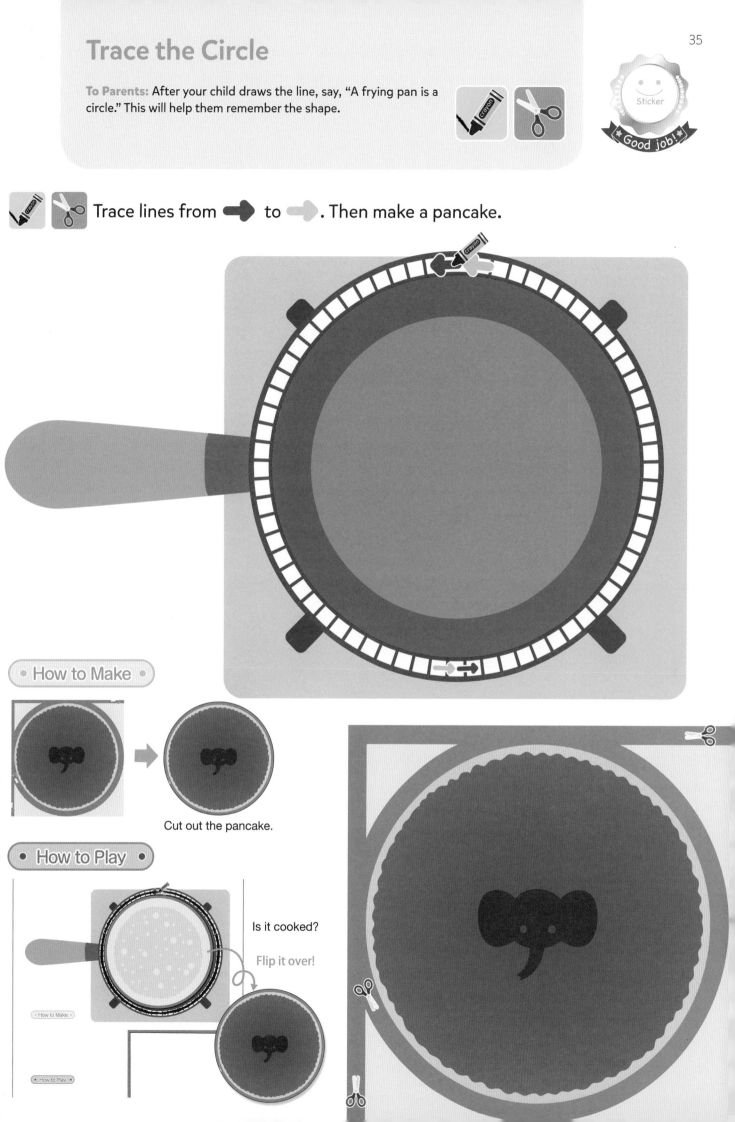

• How to Make •

Cut out the pancake.

• How to Play •

Is it cooked?

Flip it over!

35

Match Fish Patterns

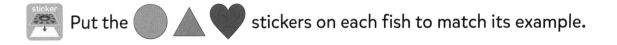 Put the ⬤ ▲ ♥ stickers on each fish to match its example.

example

Bonus Challenge! Say the name of each shape.

circle   triangle   square   heart

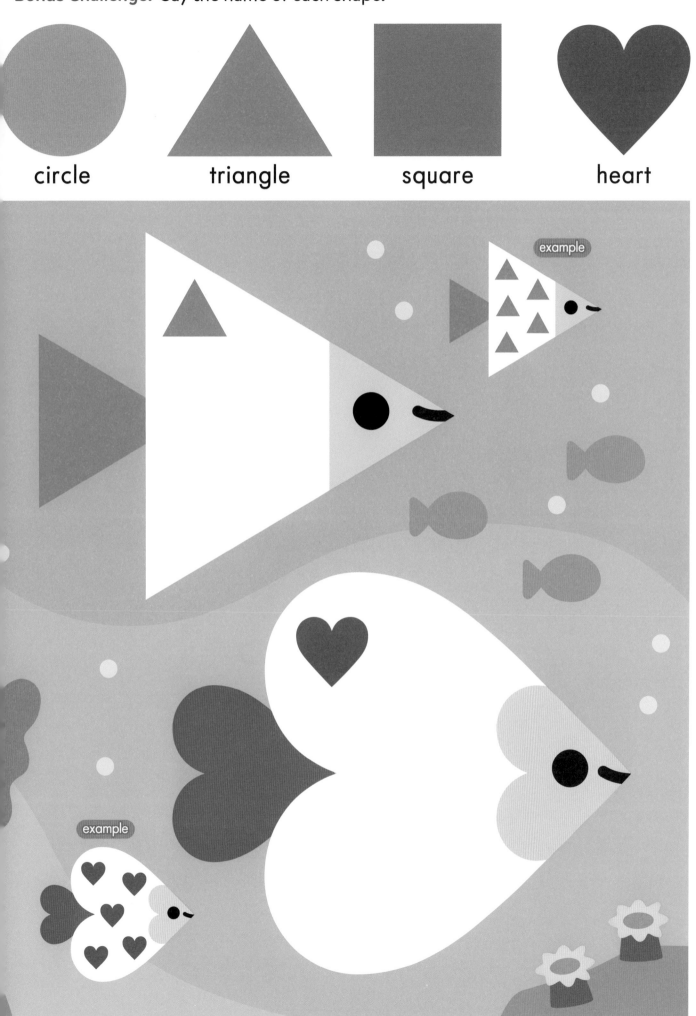

Find the Different Animal

To Parents: After your child finds the answer, ask them which part is different.

 One stuffed animal is different from the others. Find and circle it.

Brush the Bear's Teeth

To Parents: When the bear's mouth opens, let your child brush its teeth by moving the toothbrush up and down. After brushing, close the bear's mouth and say to your child, "Now the bear's teeth are clean!" Encourage your child to brush their own teeth independently. When they do, remind them to not waste water.

Sticker
Good job!

 Brush the bear's teeth.

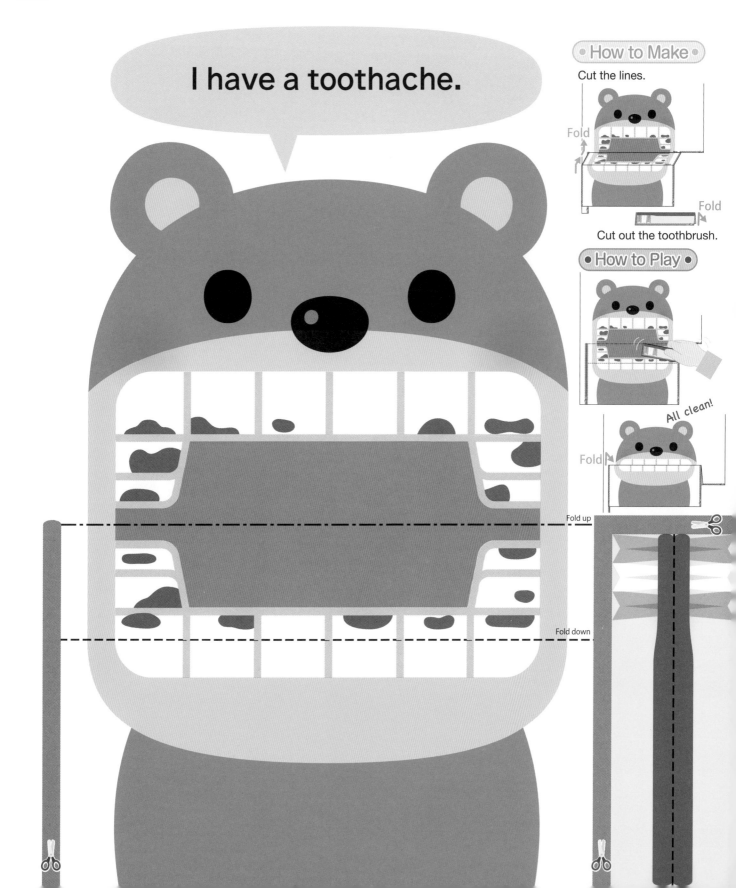

I have a toothache.

• How to Make •
Cut the lines.
Fold
Fold
Cut out the toothbrush.

• How to Play •

All clean!
Fold

Fold up
Fold down

Trace the Number 1

To Parents: Encourage your child to trace independently with a crayon. When done, play peekaboo while opening and closing the ghost.

 Trace the number 1 from ➡ to ➡. Then fold along the – – – and —·— lines. What will the ghost look like?

• How to Play •

Fold

Fold the page.
Then pull it down.

Fold down

Fold up

BOO!

Trace the Number 2

To Parents: Encourage your child to trace independently with a crayon. If they have difficulty, have them trace with a finger first. Then guide your child's hand to help them trace the number.

Trace the number 2 from  to . Then color the buses.

Good job!

Trace the Number 3

To Parents: Ask your child to say the number aloud as they trace it independently with a crayon. If they have difficulty, have them trace with a finger first.

Trace the number 3 from ➡ to ➡. Then find the sheep and put the stickers on them.

Bonus Challenge! Count the sheep and cows. Which number is more?

Count the Ducklings

To Parents: First, count the ducklings. Then fold the page for your child. After folding it, say to your child, "Look at the number 4. It's the same number as the ducklings."

Trace a line from ➡ to ➡. Count the ducklings. Then fold along the – – – and —·— lines.

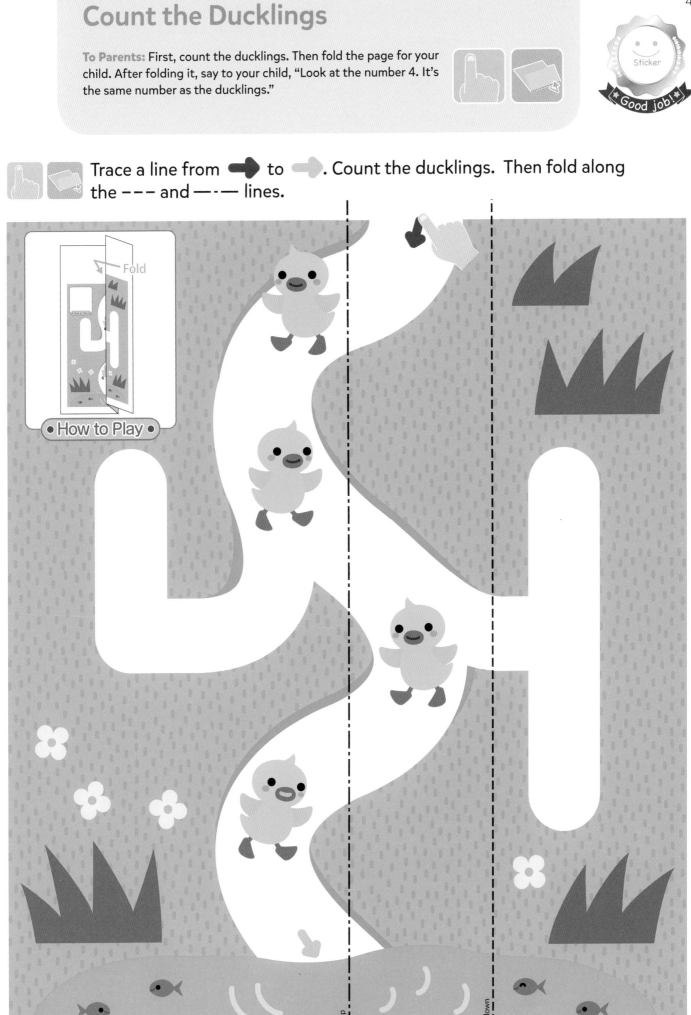

• How to Play •

Fold up

Fold down

Bonus Challenge! Count the fish and flowers.

Trace the Number 5

To Parents: The number 5 requires drawing two separate lines. Demonstrate how to draw with your finger first. Then encourage your child to try.

Trace the number 5 from ➡ to ➡. Then put a hat sticker on each child.

Bonus Challenge! Say the color of each hat.

Draw the Leaves

To Parents: This activity focuses on creativity and handwriting. Have your child draw squiggles in the white space. Don't worry if the squiggles extend outside the white space.

 Draw squiggly lines to add leaves to the tree.

example

example

Bonus Challenge! Count the birds and squirrels. Which number is more?

Sticker

Good job!

Match the Parts

To Parents: When working on matching, start with the part, then ask your child to point to the animal it's part of. Repeat this so your child can learn to make connections between a part and a whole more quickly.

 Draw a line from each animal part shown in a square below to the whole animal it's part of.

monkey

giraffe

elephant

zebra

example

Find the Hidden Objects

To Parents: When you're done, say the names of the animals: monkey, giraffe, elephant, zebra, lion, tiger, alligator, and flamingo.

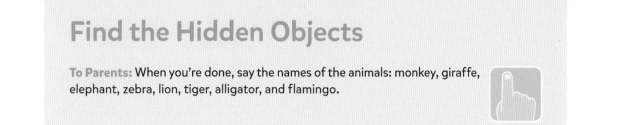

Bonus Challenge! Find a pair of scissors, a crayon, and a pencil in the pictures on pages 46 and 47.

tiger

flamingo

on

alligator

48

Draw Lines

To Parents: In this activity, your child will practice drawing curved, arched, and jagged lines. Make sure your child stops at the end of each arc and bends before moving on to the next.

Draw lines from ➡ to ➡. Then put stickers on 🔘 🔘 🔘.

Cut the Vegetables

To Parents: This activity focuses on observation skills. When your child is done, cut real vegetables to show them the differences. Talk to your child about the importance of eating healthy food.

Trace the lines from 🠶 to 🠶.
Then cut each vegetable.

• How to Make •

❶ Fold along the dotted lines.

Fold

❷ Cut along the gray lines.

Read "How to play" on page 51.

lettuce

avocado

onion

tomato

Fold up

Sticker

★ Good job! ★

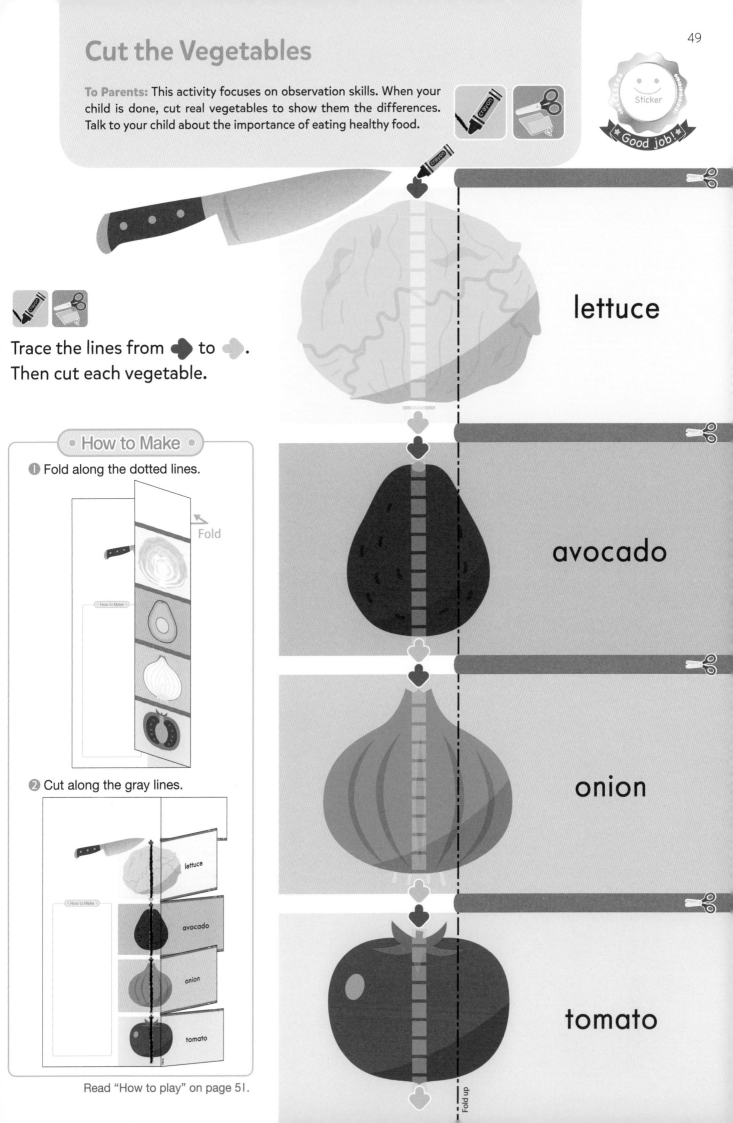

Draw Lines

Draw lines from ➡ to ➡.

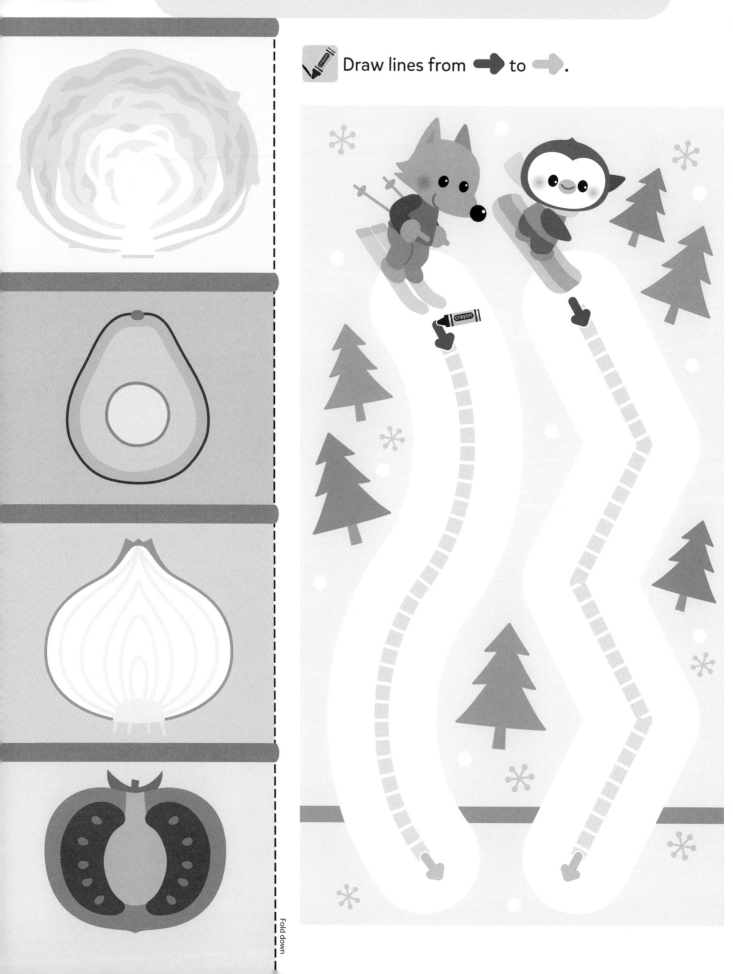

Fold down

Cut the Fruit

To Parents: This activity focuses on observation skills. When your child is done, cut real fruit to show them the differences. Talk to your child about the importance of not wasting food.

Draw lines from ◆ to ◆.
Then cut each fruit.

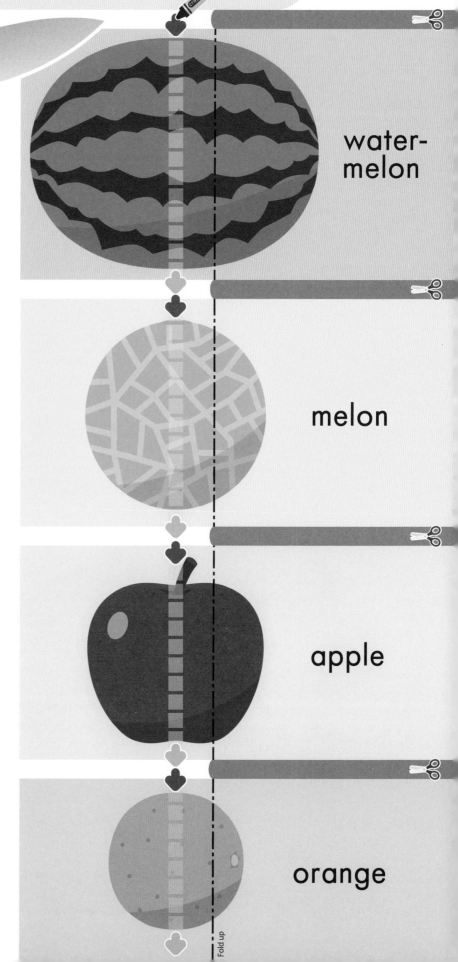

water-melon

melon

apple

orange

• How to Play •

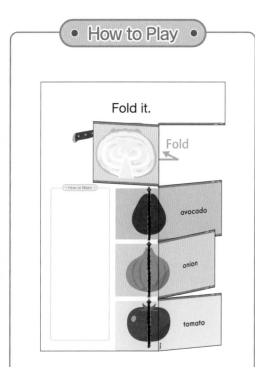

Fold it.

Look at each folded vegetable.
Guess the vegetables. Do the
same with the fruits.

52

Draw Lines

To Parents: Have your child use the dotted line only as a guide. It is more important for your child to draw a curved line in one continuous movement than it is to follow the dotted line exactly.

Draw a line from ➡ to ➡. Color the pig pink.

Bonus Challenge! Count the bees and flowers. Which number is more?

Fold down

Follow the Police Cars

To Parents: This activity is designed to help your child recognize objects that are the same. Encourage your child to first trace with their finger, then let them do it with a crayon.

Follow the police cars with your finger to get from ➡ to ➡.

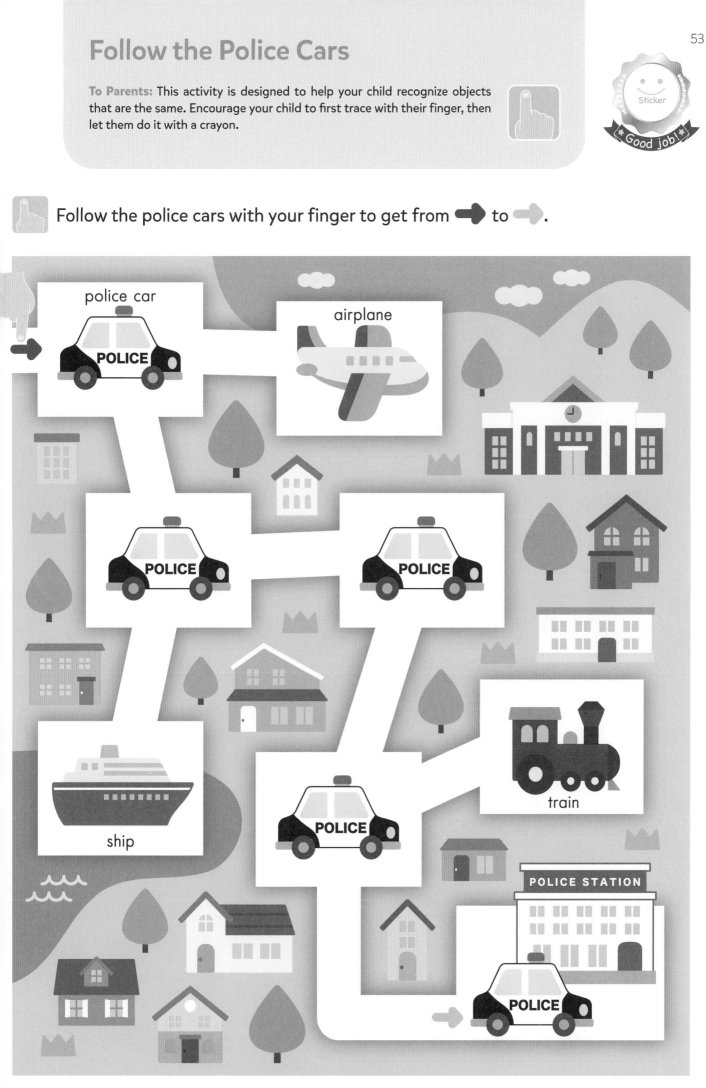

Bonus Challenge! Say the name of each vehicle.

Spot the Differences

To Parents: In this activity, your child will practice finding differences between two similar pictures. Help your child by providing hints, if needed. These are the items that are different in the bottom picture: tomato, hamburger, and plate. Talk to your child about helping clean up when they are done with a meal.

Find three differences between the two pictures below. Put a ● sticker on each difference in the bottom picture.

Spot the Differences

To Parents: If this activity seems difficult, provide hints for your child. These are the items that are different in the bottom picture: panda, car, and yellow block. Encourage your child to put away their toys independently when they are done playing.

 Find three differences between the two pictures below. Put a ⬤ sticker on each difference in the bottom picture.

Make Shapes

To Parents: When your child is making a rectangle, make sure they reverse one hand. Also, encourage your child to say the name of each shape they make with their hands. This will help them learn shape recognition.

 Make shapes with your fingers. Then say the name of each shape.

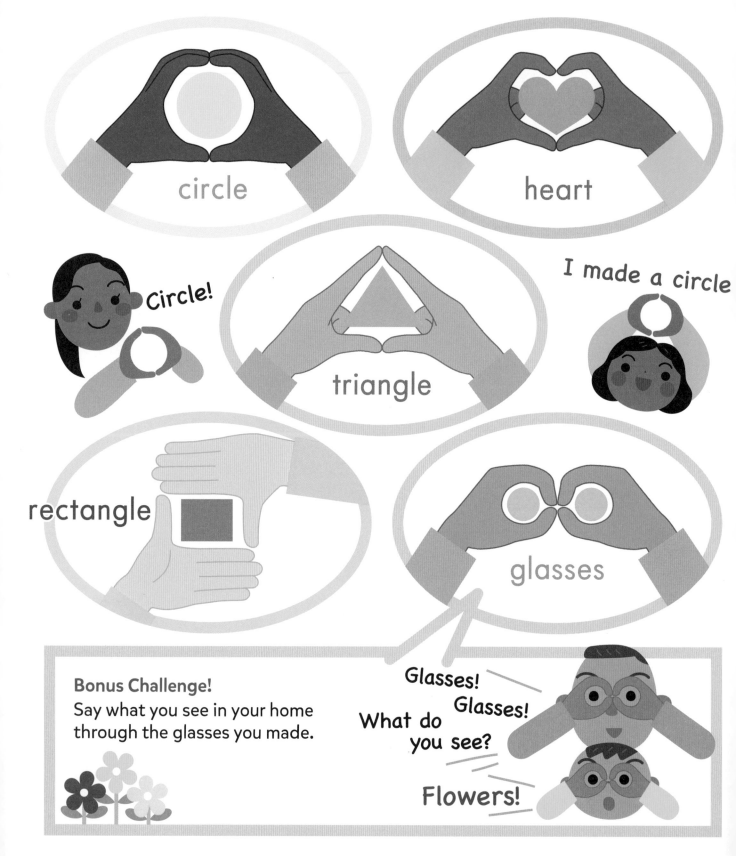

circle

heart

Circle!

triangle

I made a circle

rectangle

glasses

Bonus Challenge!
Say what you see in your home through the glasses you made.

Glasses! Glasses!
What do you see?

Flowers!

Make Clouds

57

To Parents: Let your child tear the cloud paper into different shapes. Then encourage them to glue the cloud pieces to the sky. When complete, tell them, "The clouds seem to be moving slowly."

Cut out the paper below. Tear it into cloud shapes. Then glue the clouds to the sky.

example

Complete the Picture

To Parents: In this activity, your child will build spatial reasoning skills by using the puzzle pieces to fill in the missing part of the picture. Ask your child when the other tool is used. When done, show your child how to take care of any plants in your home.

 Complete the picture. Find the picture to fill in the ▇ and color the ◯ below it.

Find Animals

To Parents: In this activity, your child will develop observation and concentration skills. After completing the "Bonus Challenge!" activity, draw eyes and a mouth so each animal matches the example. If there are pets in your home, show your child how to care for them.

Find animals hidden in the picture and color the ◯ below the animal when you find it.

Bonus Challenge! Color and identify the animals you find.

Complete the Picture

 Complete the picture. Find the picture to fill in the ☐ and color the ◯ below it.

Complete the Picture

To Parents: Have your child match the pieces by paying attention to the colors of the slide, dog, and house.

 Cut out the pictures below. Then glue them onto the [paste] to complete the picture.

Bonus Challenge! Count the birds.

62

Find the Matching Shirts

To Parents: This activity focuses on recognizing the similarities and differences among objects. If your child is having a hard time finding the matches, point out the colors and patterns of the clothes.

Draw a line to connect the matching shirts.

example

glue   glue   glue

Find the Same Animal

To Parents: After your child successfully names the animals, quiz them by saying, "Who says baa, baa?"

Draw a line from each animal to its match at the bottom of the page.

farmer

cow

dog

cat

duck

horse

goat

sheep

example

chick

hen

pig

mouse

rabbit

Bonus Challenge! Say the name of each animal.

Connect the Dots

To Parents: To begin, count the numbers 1 to 10 aloud with your child. Then ask them to trace from dot to dot with their finger as you count.

 Connect the dots in order from 1 to 10.

Go Green Activity Board

Draw fruits and vegetables like the examples.

To Parents: The fruits and vegetables that support our healthy lifestyles grow in different places, such as in the soil and on trees. Ask your child where they've seen food growing.

Use water-based markers on this side of the board. When your child is finished drawing, erase the board with a damp cloth or a tissue.

Then, find the bottle and can and circle them.

To Parents: Ask your child where animals live, such as in a meadow, pasture, or pond. Tell them, "Creatures live together with humans on earth. When we pollute their homes by dumping garbage, these creatures are affected, so we must try to keep our earth clean and healthy."